save the . . .
KOALAS

by **Anita Sanchez**
with an introduction
by **Chelsea Clinton**

PHILOMEL

To Sam, Corey, and Mercedes: my furry buddies

PHILOMEL
An imprint of Penguin Random House LLC, New York

First published in the United States of America by Philomel,
an imprint of Penguin Random House LLC, 2023

Text copyright © 2023 by Chelsea Clinton

Photo credits: page 2: © rueangrit/Adobe Stock; page 5: © Rafael Ben-Ari/Adobe Stock;
page 7: © AUFORT/Adobe Stock; page 13: © peter_qn/Adobe Stock; page 19:
© Greg Brave/Adobe Stock; page 23: MrPreecha/Adobe Stock; page 25: © Pascal/
Adobe Stock; page 32: © Bettapoggi/Adobe Stock; page 34: © bennymarty/Adobe Stock;
page 36–37: © Bumble Dee/Adobe Stock; page 39: © toa555/Adobe Stock; page 41:
© robdthebaker/Adobe Stock; page 47: © MrPreecha/Adobe Stock; page 50: © Tanya/
Adobe Stock; page 53: © jean-michel delage/EyeEm/Adobe Stock; page 55:
© jean-michel delage/EyeEm/Adobe Stock; page 62: © Australian Koala Foundation;
page 67: © dangdumrong/Adobe Stock

Philomel is a registered trademark of Penguin Random House LLC.
The Penguin colophon is a registered trademark of Penguin Books Limited.

Visit us online at PenguinRandomHouse.com.

Library of Congress Cataloging-in-Publication Data is available.

ISBN 9780593622636 (hardcover)
ISBN 9780593622643 (paperback)

1st Printing

Printed in the United States of America

LSCC

Edited by Talia Benamy and Jill Santopolo • Design by Lily Qian
Text set in Calisto MT Pro

save the . . .

save the . . .
BLUE WHALES

save the . . .
ELEPHANTS

save the . . .
FROGS

save the . . .
GIRAFFES

save the . . .
GORILLAS

save the . . .
KOALAS

save the . . .
LIONS

save the . . .
POLAR BEARS

save the . . .
RHINOCEROSES

save the . . .
TIGERS

save the . . .
WHALE SHARKS

Dear Reader,

When I was around your age, my favorite animals were dinosaurs and elephants. I wanted to know everything I could about triceratopses, stegosauruses and other dinosaurs that had roamed our earth millions of years ago. Elephants, though, captured my curiosity and my heart. The more I learned about the largest animals on land today, the more I wanted to do to help keep them and other endangered species safe forever.

So I joined organizations working around the world to support endangered species and went to our local zoo to learn more about conservation efforts close to home (thanks to my parents and grandparents). I tried to learn as much as I could about how we can ensure animals and plants don't go extinct like the dinosaurs, especially since it's the choices that we're making that pose the greatest threat to their lives today.

The choices we make don't have to be huge to make

a real difference. When I was in elementary school, I used to cut up the plastic rings around six-packs of soda, glue them to brightly colored construction paper (purple was my favorite) and hand them out to whomever would take one in a one-girl campaign to raise awareness about the dangers that plastic six-pack rings posed to marine wildlife around the world. I learned about that from a book—*50 Simple Things Kids Can Do to Save the Earth*—which helped me understand that you're never too young to make a difference and that we all can change the world. I hope that this book will inform and inspire you to help save this and other endangered species. There are tens of thousands of species that are currently under threat, with more added every year. We have the power to save those species, and with your help, we can.

Sincerely,

Chelsea Clinton

save the . . .
KOALAS

CONTENTS

1

LIFE IN THE POISON FOREST

Have you ever hugged a koala bear? You might have! A lot of the stuffed teddy bears you see on toy store shelves are designed to look like cute, fuzzy koalas. But in real life, there's no such thing as a koala bear.

The small mammals known as koalas are often called bears because they look like little bear cubs with their short, round ears, pudgy bodies, and stubby noses. But koalas aren't related to bears at all—they're a special kind of animal called a marsupial, which means that they carry their babies in a pouch on their stomachs. These funny, furry animals are some of the most amazing creatures that live on the huge island-continent of Australia.

Koalas are like no other animal on Earth.

The Boy Who Fell from the Tree

Since Australia is not connected by land to any other continents, the animals there evolved to be very different from the creatures found everywhere else in the world—it has fascinating creatures like kangaroos, wombats, duck-billed platypuses, and koalas. Koalas have lived in Australia for a long, long time. People searching in the rocks of Australia have found fossils of koala-like animals that might be more than twenty million years old.

That means koalas were living in Australia long, long before people arrived. Humans probably came to Australia about fifty thousand years ago. No one knows exactly where these adventurous people came from, but they must have crossed the wide, dangerous seas in boats. And once they did, they found a land filled with forests, with millions of koalas living high in the treetops.

These first people to arrive on the mainland,

known as Aboriginal peoples, were the only humans who lived in Australia for tens of thousands of years. Their stories about how the earth was created and shaped are called the Dreamings, and they describe how the rocks, plants, animals, and everything else fit together. Over the centuries, they have told many tales about the wise-eyed creatures that clamber in the branches over their heads. Thousands of years ago, they gave these animals the name koo-la, which means "no water." Those long-ago storytellers had observed a very unusual thing about koalas—they almost never drink!

According to one legend, there was once a boy who lived in a dry land. His enemies refused to share their water and wouldn't let him drink from the ponds or streams. But one day he had an idea—he hung buckets of water high in the

Descendants of the first peoples who came to Australia still tell stories of the Dreamings.

branches of trees so that he would always have enough to drink. Sadly, he fell from the tree-tops, but his body was magically healed and turned into a koala. The water he had hidden in the trees flowed into the leaves.

Koalas need water to survive, of course, as all living things do. But unlike most other land mammals, they can get the water they need from the moisture in the plants they eat. They only climb down from their treetops to search for water during a heat wave, or if they can't find enough juicy leaves.

The Trees of Life

Trees are koalas' life-giving habitat. Trees provide them with food, water, a place to sleep, and a home to shelter their babies. But koalas won't feed on just any kind of tree. Koalas are very, very picky about what kinds of leaves they eat.

Koalas eat almost nothing but the leaves of eucalyptus trees, which are evergreens with long pointed leaves that are glossy green. (Evergreens are plants that stay green all year long.) These trees have oily sap that is as sticky as gum, and Australians often call them gum trees. (If you've ever sung "Kookaburra sits in the old gum tree," you were singing about the koalas' favorite tree.)

But even once they find gum trees, koalas are still pretty picky. There are more than seven hundred species of eucalyptus, and the fussy koalas will eat leaves from only about a dozen of those. Koalas have to find just the right kind

Koala noses sniff out just the right leaves to munch on.

of tree before they climb up and start snacking. Those cute black noses have a keen sense of smell, and a koala can tell if a tree is the right kind just by sniffing it.

Eucalyptus forests make up about three-quarters of Australia's total forest land. They thrive in the hot, dry climate and can grow even in soil that doesn't have a lot of nutrients in it. And these shaggy, scraggly-looking trees have a wonderful secret. If you rub one of the leathery leaves, it gives off a strong scent that's hard to describe—sort of minty, fresh, and clean, but also spicy. You might have smelled it when you had a cold, as it's found in many different kinds of cough drops and cold remedies. (If you want to know what a gum tree smells like, sniff a jar of Vicks VapoRub.) Aboriginal peoples honor the eucalyptus as a special tree with healing powers. And modern medical research has shown that they're right! Eucalyptus does help to kill germs and to clear a stuffy nose or chest.

For koalas, the best thing about feeding on eucalyptus leaves is that few other kinds of animals eat them. Wombats—a type of Australian mammal that looks a bit like a short-legged, fat koala—will also eat eucalyptus leaves, but wombats live on the ground, not high in trees. Even most insects don't eat gum tree leaves—the strong scent is the tree's way of discouraging bugs from nibbling the leaves. So koalas have little competition at mealtimes.

Here's another reason that koalas don't have much competition for their meals: eucalyptus leaves contain a powerful poison! The oily juice found in the leaves contains several powerful chemicals that are harmful to most mammals. Just one teaspoon of pure eucalyptus oil could kill a person. (When humans use it as a medicine, only tiny amounts are given.) This powerful toxin is the way the tree protects itself—if eucalyptus leaves were sweet and delicious, they'd soon be gobbled up by many different creatures. But how can koalas eagerly munch on leaves that would make another mammal drop dead? The answer lies inside the koala's furry tummy.

All mammals (including people) have a body part called a liver that acts like a filter, straining harmful substances from the blood. But koalas have what some scientists call a "super liver" that is especially good at removing the eucalyptus toxins as they pass through the animal's body. Koalas can eat the leaves without so much as a stomachache. The toxins are strained out of the bloodstream and leave the koala's body in its urine.

Life in the Slow Lane

But wait, there's another reason that most other animals don't try to eat eucalyptus leaves. Not only are they toxic, they're also low in nutrition. Most foods that wild animals seek out are filled with nutrients to give them energy and help them grow strong. People need nutritious food, too. When you eat a leaf of spinach, for example, it gives you protein, iron, calcium, vitamins, and lots of other things your body needs. But eucalyptus leaves are very low in nutrients. And, like most leaves, they're also low-calorie, which means they don't provide much energy.

Once again, the solution lies inside the

incredible koala stomach. Koalas have a really long digestive system, much longer than that of other animals their size. It's full of twists and turns, where the tough eucalyptus leaves are slowly broken down by stomach acids so that every ounce of nutrition can be used by the animal.

But because they eat such a low-calorie food, koalas have little energy to spare. Almost everything koalas do is slow. They'll spend hours in the same tree, choosing and munching leaves. Then they'll slowly clamber down from the tree, bottom-first. When they find a promising new tree, they climb up and start to eat again. Koalas eat almost every minute that they're awake—but that's not for long. As soon as koalas are full, they fall asleep. Sometimes they even doze off while chewing. Those long,

Naptime!

curved claws help the koala cling tight to branches, even in their sleep.

And koalas sleep a lot—often about twenty hours a day. They crouch in the branches, dozing all day and most of the night. They sometimes poop in their sleep! As soon as they wake up, it's back to eating—they can chew their way through about a pound of leaves in a day. Then it's time to nap again.

Imagine sleeping for twenty hours while sitting on a gnarly tree branch. Doesn't sound comfortable! But koalas are well built for a life spent sitting—they have extra-thick fur padding their bottoms, making a soft pillow to sit on. Their fuzzy bottoms are speckled gray and white, so they blend in with the shadows of leaves and branches, making the koalas hard to spot on their high perches. So if you went for a hike in an Australian eucalyptus forest, you'd have a hard time spotting a koala—unless you knew where to look!

2

THE ROAR OF THE KOALA

As you wander through a eucalyptus forest, the trees reach high over your head, the scent of their leaves strong in the hot sun. You might hear the chatter of nesting kookaburras or the squawk of parrots. You might see lizards sunning themselves on a branch or even glimpse a kangaroo hopping away. And if you looked up, of course, you might see a koala sitting high in the treetops.

All koalas look alike—at first glance. But if

you look closely, you'll see that they are different from each other. Male koalas are bigger, with the biggest weighing twenty-five pounds or so—about as much as a mid-size dog. Females are smaller, generally five pounds lighter. But, like people, some individual koalas grow bigger than others. Also, koala faces aren't all the same—some have smaller noses or differently shaped eyes or ears, and they have different expressions. And, just like people, each individual koala has its own special personality.

Deborah Tabart is the head of the Australian Koala Foundation, which works to protect koalas. She says, "Every koala I have known is different from the rest and, like humans, have their own way of doing things. There have been grumpy koalas and happy koalas." Some koalas are timid; others are more aggressive.

Some are curious about exploring new places and trying new things; others are content to stay close to the same few trees.

Koalas travel from tree to tree within an area called a home range. Depending on how many eucalyptus trees there are in the area, the range varies in size. In a national park, where the gum trees grow densely, the koalas' ranges are smaller, since they don't have to travel as far to find food. But in areas outside of parks, where houses and roads are in between patches of trees, a koala might need a range as large as 250 acres. That's about the size of sixty city blocks. A koala will usually live its whole life within its range, just moving from tree to tree when the leaf supply runs low.

Koalas rarely spend time hanging out together. They tend to stay in their own separate trees. The male, called a buck, definitely doesn't want other bucks around—he guards his territory carefully and tries to keep other males out. He does this by two ways: smell and sound.

Male koalas have a scent gland in the middle of their chests. This is a patch of bare skin that oozes out a smelly, sticky substance This leaves a round brown stain in the middle of his chest, which is a handy way to tell males from females. The buck will rub his chest on the base of trees in his home range, and the smell will last for many days. The strong odor tells other males: *This is MY tree. Stay away!*

Male koalas also defend their territory with the power of their voices. When it's time to find a mate in the spring, the bucks give off incredibly loud bellows. The noises that these cuddly-looking little animals make are so ferocious

The love song of the koala can be heard far and wide.

that when moviemakers needed sound effects for the rampaging *Tyrannosaurus rex* in the movie *Jurassic Park*, what did they use? Tape-recorded koala calls! A male koala can give off earsplitting roars that can be heard half a mile away.

Koalas only mate once a year. No need to waste energy swinging through trees looking for mates—the bucks just shout out their deafening love song. The does are attracted to the males with the loudest roars. Their keen sense of smell lets the females sniff out exactly which tree the male is calling from.

A Very Unusual Baby

After the male and female mate, the male goes back to his loud signaling. A buck might mate with several does in a single year, but he doesn't take part in raising any of the young koalas.

The female koala doesn't have long to wait before the baby is born. Koala mothers are only pregnant for about thirty-five days. You'd think a newborn koala, called a joey, would be adorable—but turns out the tiny newcomer is not exactly cute! It's just a small pink blob about the size of a jelly bean. It weighs approximately one gram, which is the weight of a small paper clip. The infant is completely helpless and can barely move. It hasn't yet grown fur, eyes, or ears—but it does have a nose.

The joey sniffs and wriggles, and then slowly begins its long journey along the mother's stomach. The tiny, determined infant pushes its way through her thick fur until finally it struggles to the opening of a warm, welcoming pouch. There in the cozy darkness, the baby is safely tucked away as it continues to grow and develop for many months. While living in the pouch, it nurses milk from its mother.

After many weeks, the baby starts poking its head out of the mother's pouch and peering with round black eyes at the big world out there. At first, things are too bright and scary after the safe darkness. Quickly it dives back into the pouch! It takes about six months before the baby is ready to venture out of the safe pouch. Then the mother feeds it a special kind of baby food.

She does this by chewing up some leaves and then partly digesting them in her own stomach. They come out as a kind of poop, soft and mushy like baby food, and the joey gobbles it down. This weird food is called pap, and it helps the baby get ready to eat on its own. Within a few months, the joey is nibbling on its first few leaves.

The mother and baby share a close bond. Usually it's an "only child," since twins are rare. The mother chooses tender leaves to hand to her baby, and by watching mom, the youngster learns to find just the right leaves to eat. When it's time to move to a new tree, the joey

Baby joey holds on tight.

will cling to mom's back, holding tightly to her fur as she travels.

The baby that was once the size of a paper clip grows fast! By the time it's six months old, a joey is about the size of a house cat. The youngster gets braver and braver about venturing farther from mom, although the "teenager" will often return for a hug and a cuddle. Finally, after a year or more, the young koala is ready to strike out on its own. Only then will the mother be ready to mate again. She doesn't have a baby every year, but over the course of her lifetime, a doe might have four or five babies.

Young female koalas tend to stay close to home, hanging out in trees near where they grew up. Sometimes they will travel a bit, especially if food is scarce, but they often end up not far from where they started. But if the youngster is a male, it will probably go looking for a new home range where it can find females to mate with. It can be hard for young koalas to find a spot, since full-grown males will defend their home ranges from other males. A koala guarding his territory will roar fiercely to scare off the intruder. If that doesn't work, the males will sometimes fight, wrestling and punching each other with long claws bared, screeching in fury.

Koalas may be cute, but they can be fierce, too!

It can take a long time for a young buck to find a home. But after months of exploring, he may find just the right place with enough food trees, perhaps some water nearby, and a few females to mate with. Then new koala families will begin, and the cycle of life starts anew.

What's a Koala Thinking About?

A koala sits munching on a eucalyptus leaf, chewing steadily while it stares into space.

Then it blinks and eats another leaf. Koalas seem to lead a quiet life, filled with nothing but eating and sleeping. Compared to their body size, their brains are quite small. For a long time, most people assumed that koalas, although cute, were not very smart animals. But now wildlife researchers are starting to discover that there's a lot going on behind those sleepy eyes.

A busy highway in an area of Australia called Queensland cuts between two forested areas that are prime koala habitat. The traffic-filled road was a dangerous place for wildlife. So the Queenslanders invented ways to help animals cross the road safely, building tunnels and overpasses.

Many people doubted that these passage-ways would be of any use to koalas. Surely, they thought, koalas wouldn't be smart enough to figure out anything new.

But the koalas surprised everyone. Within months, they were experts at using the new routes. They explored the tunnels and bridges and learned to balance on narrow ledges. "No koala has ever walked under a road on a ledge ever before in its evolutionary history," said Professor Darryl Jones, who helped design the crossings. "This proves they really can innovate" (which means they can try new things).

One thing is for sure: koalas have figured out how to survive in a challenging habitat that few other animals can use. Koalas' history goes back a long way—they've been a part of the Australian landscape for millions of years.

But what lies ahead for the koalas' future?

3

HOW MANY KOALAS?

When the first Europeans arrived in Australia, there were literally millions of koalas living in the forests that spread all across the continent. The newcomers ruthlessly displaced the Aboriginal peoples and took over their ancient lands. The Europeans soon discovered that the koalas' thick fur was soft, warm, and highly waterproof, and that it made excellent gloves, hats, and linings for coats. Soon there was an enormous trade in koala furs, which meant hunters killed koalas in huge numbers. Few people worried about running out of koalas— there were so many it seemed as though they would always be there. From 1888 to 1927, more than eight million koala skins were shipped out of Australia.

It took many years before people noticed that koala populations were getting smaller and smaller. Finally, laws were passed to ban the hunting of them. And people began to realize that many other species of wildlife all over the world were in danger of disappearing too.

So a group of scientists started an organization called the International Union for Conservation of Nature (IUCN). This group has a list, called the IUCN Red List of Threatened Species™, which keeps track of all the endangered species of animals and plants (and even fungi!) in the whole world. The animals are put into seven categories to show levels of threat. Least Concern and Near Threatened mean that the animals are pretty much all right, but we need to keep an eye on them. Vulnerable means that there are problems that could soon cause the species to become Endangered. Endangered and Critically Endangered mean that populations of these creatures are dropping fast and need help soon to ensure their survival. Extinct in the Wild means the animal exists only in captivity. And once a species is listed as Extinct, it's too late to help them anymore. They're gone forever.

For more than twenty years, koalas were on the Red List as Least Concern. But even so, many people in Australia who love koalas were worried about the beloved furry animals. The trade in koala pelts had stopped, but the eucalyptus trees that koalas need for habitat were disappearing fast.

Dense, shady eucalyptus forests once covered large portions of the Australian continent. But over the centuries the forests have shrunk as more and more trees are cut down for lumber, or to make products like paper towels, paper plates, or toilet paper. Forest land is also often cleared to make room for houses, roads, farms, or mines. Now eucalyptus forests—and koalas—are mostly found in a narrow belt along the eastern coast, in Queensland and New South Wales.

Koalas have become a symbol of Australia, their teddy-bear faces known all over the world. Millions of people love to see koalas in zoos, and if they're lucky enough, to spot them in the wild. When important people visit Australia, they're often photographed holding a koala.

President Obama, Queen Elizabeth II, and Pope John Paul II have all cuddled koalas for the camera. (Now, though, it is illegal in most of Australia to hug a koala unless you are a trained wildlife ranger, although visitors are often still allowed to touch a koala in a supervised setting. These rules are to protect koalas' safety and well-being.)

But what if someday there weren't any more koalas?

As the twenty-first century dawned, koalas no longer numbered in the millions. Koalas were uplisted to Vulnerable on the Red List in 2014, and as the destruction of their habitat continued, their numbers continued to drop. The poison forest that gives life to the koalas was getting smaller every year.

Left: The poisonous forest gives life to koalas.

Can you spot the koala?

The well-camouflaged koalas, dozing high in the treetops, are hard to spot. So it's difficult for researchers to know exactly how many there are. In 2018, wildlife biologists estimated that there were probably only about eighty thousand koalas left.

But then, in 2019, a disaster began to unfold that changed Australia in a terrifying way. After that long, dreadful Black Summer, the koalas' world would never be the same again.

Fire!

The spring of 2019 had been an unusually hot and dry one across the whole Australian continent. Little rain had fallen. Rivers and streams were low, and water holes had vanished. The soil was dusty and bone-dry. In the eucalyptus forests, piles of brown, crunchy leaves lay under the wilting trees. In June, the fire service warned people that the usual season of brush fires could be starting early that year.

Fire has long been a part of Australian life. During the dry season, usually from July to October, brush fires frequently burn across grasslands and forests. Eucalyptus trees are well adapted to survive a small fire that burns up dried leaves and twigs but passes quickly. A few smaller trees might be damaged, but the big, tall trees aren't killed. They have thick, fire-resistant bark to guard them from the heat. In fact, the seeds of some types of gum trees are carried inside a cone that's sealed with a sticky sap called resin, and the seeds can't start growing until a fire has melted the resin.

But that year, the fires started much earlier in the dry season. They lasted longer, covering more ground than usual. And soon the fires were blazing more fiercely than they ever had before.

Fire!

A Change in the Air

Pollution caused by human inventions like cars, power plants, and factories has been changing Earth's atmosphere and has caused temperatures around the world to rise. Australia is already a hot and dry country, so the effects of climate change are hitting there sooner than in other countries with cooler, wetter climates. The increased heat and droughts are causing more and more savage wildfires.

In 2019, the land was so dry that almost

anything could start a fire: a lightning strike, a carelessly dropped match, a spark from a firecracker. And these fires were incredibly powerful. These intense blazes didn't simply scorch the eucalyptus trees, helping their seeds to open. These fires burned cones, seeds, leaves, and branches. The oily sap that fills eucalyptus trees burned fiercely, turning whole trees into giant torches.

The Black Summer

The wildfires burned on and on for months into 2020. Record high temperatures dried the land out even more. The thermometer was over 100°F for days on end. On the worst day, the temperature hit 120°F. The fires blazed near towns and cities, destroying homes and stores. Choking billows of smoke darkened the skies and sent thousands of people to the hospital.

Dr. Rebecca Montague-Drake, one of the staff at a wildlife organization called Koala Recovery Partnership, recalled what it was like. "This

Firefighters battled the flames all through the Black Summer.

summer brought the reality of what it is like to live with intense water restrictions, heat, and fire home to us," she said. "Many of us became 'climate refugees' as we evacuated our houses until the bushfire threat had passed (some poor people of course had no home to return to) or because we had simply run out of water."

For wildlife, the flames brought disaster. The massive fires roared over the dry ground so fast that even kangaroos couldn't flee out of the path of the flames. Birds trying to fly away fell dead from the heat. Slow-moving koalas had no way to escape. It's estimated that billions of animals died. The worst part of the fires fell in summer of 2020, and Australians will forever after remember it as the Black Summer. Finally, though, rains came, and the fires slowly died away, leaving a blackened, lifeless landscape.

A Shrinking Home

Koalas were especially hard-hit by the devastating wildfires. More than seventy million acres burned, and a billion trees were destroyed. A third of koalas' habitat was lost. And even now as the koalas struggle to recover from the fires, their habitat is still being lost. Every time a patch of gum trees is cut down to make room

No tree, no me.

for another house or a grove of trees is flattened by a new road, koalas lose a little more of their home.

And it's not just that their homes and sources of food are being destroyed—there are other dangers to koalas from habitat loss. When people build their houses in koala habitats, even if some trees are left standing, it's tough for the animals to survive. They have to come down from their trees sometimes to find a new tree with fresh leaves or to search for a mate. And as soon as they reach the ground, they're in danger.

In the wild, koalas have few predators. Occasionally, wild dogs called dingoes will catch one, or a hawk or eagle might swoop down and grab a joey. But koalas' most serious threats come from people—even if those people don't mean to harm them.

Slow-moving koalas trying to cross roads often get hit by cars. They mostly move at night, so drivers don't see them until it's too late. Sometimes they're chased or attacked by people's pet dogs. Koalas can move fast if they feel threatened—they can run faster than a human—but only for short distances. Running uses up a lot of precious energy. Even a friendly dog trying to play can exhaust a koala, and some dogs will bite or even kill them. Sometimes koalas fall into swimming pools and drown. All sorts of things we take for granted in a neighborhood—roads, fences, pets, backyard pools—are threats to a koala trying to make its way to a new tree.

A Disease That's Hard to Cure

Koalas also can get a serious disease called chlamydia. This is a bacterial infection that koalas probably originally caught from sheep or cows many years ago when European farmers first began to move into koala territory. Chlamydia is contagious and is spread from one koala to another when they mate, or from mother to baby. It affects the koalas' reproductive organs, making it harder for them to have babies. It can also affect their eyes, causing blindness.

Veterinarians have been searching for a cure for koala chlamydia for many years. Since it's caused by bacteria, medicines called antibiotics should be able to cure it, just like you might take antibiotics to cure strep throat or an ear infection. In fact, if humans get chlamydia, they can take antibiotics. But here's where the koala's unusual stomach doesn't help it. The bacteria in their systems, which are so good at coping with eucalyptus leaves, are damaged by antibiotics, making it difficult for the animals to get the nutrition they need. So the medicine that can be so helpful to us can actually wind up hurting koalas in the long run.

Chlamydia is not usually fatal if a strong, healthy animal comes down with it. But if the animal is already weak, stressed by hunger or thirst, the disease will weaken them further. Koalas living in protected areas like parks or nature centers are better able to resist the disease. But in areas where their food trees are burned or cut down, they are much harder hit by the effects of the sickness.

In 2021, researchers began giving koalas a vaccine that can prevent them from getting the disease—or, if they do get it, to have a much less serious case. The problem is that it's hard to vaccinate a patient that's sitting on a branch high overhead! So far only a few wild koalas have received the vaccine. But as more and more animals get the shot, the vaccine will help to make chlamydia less of a threat to koalas.

Downward Trend

Deborah Tabart from the Australian Koala Foundation is angry about what's happening to her favorite animal's habitat. "I have seen some landscapes that look like the moon—with dead and dying trees everywhere," she says. "Urgent action to stop land clearing in prime koala habitat is required if we are to save our beloved national animal."

Since 2018, koalas have lost about a third of their population. It's very hard to be sure exactly how many there are left, but in 2022, the Australian Koala Foundation estimated there were perhaps as few as thirty-two thousand. In every area where koalas are found, their numbers are going down each year. Although the koala remains listed as Vulnerable on the Red List, many wildlife biologists are warning that it should be considered as Endangered. Koalas were officially declared to be an endangered species by some of the Australian states in 2021.

What's Next?

Across millions of Australian acres, the blackened earth seemed lifeless after the fires had

Koalas are looking to us for support.

swept across it. But as time passed, green shoots began to push through the ashes. Charred gum trees put forth new sprouts. Seeds of new trees start to grow. The forest is slowly coming back to life. And people all over the world are coming together to find ways to save the koalas.

Even dogs are pitching in to help.

4

UP FROM THE ASHES

Across the ashes of a burned forest comes a small four-legged creature. It wanders between charred eucalyptus stumps, sniffing the blackened ground. The animal is brown and furry, and on its paws, it wears little red booties.

Wait. *Little red booties?*

The creature with the unusual footwear is not a koala, it's a Koolie. A Koolie is a breed of Australian dog with lots of energy and a keen sense of smell. This makes them perfect to be wildlife search-and-rescue dogs.

Bear is a six-year-old Koolie who has spent many hours searching burned forests for injured koalas. The booties he wears keep his paws from being hurt by hot embers or sharp stones. Bear works long hours roaming burned areas, and

Koolie dogs' keen noses sniff out koalas.

he has sniffed out more than a hundred koalas. To him, tracking down koalas is a game. When he finds a koala, he's praised and given treats. He doesn't realize that his koala-finding game is helping to save an endangered species.

It's hard to find the well-camouflaged koalas anytime, but it's especially difficult for humans to spot them after a fire. Their smoke-blackened fur blends in perfectly with the charred tree trunks. In spite of the fact that they're capable of making earsplitting noises, when a koala is injured, it tends to huddle quietly.

So after a brush fire has swept through a forest, rescue dogs are brought to the area by handlers who have trained the dogs to seek out the special scent of koalas. If a koala is up in a tree, the dog will lie down at the bottom so the handlers know which tree to search.

And it's not only dogs who are on the alert for koalas. All across southeastern Australia, volunteers spend hours peering into thickets and gazing up at treetops, scouring the burned lands for koalas.

When a koala is found, it's gently examined to see if it needs help. Most koalas in burned areas are badly dehydrated, meaning that their bodies are desperately in need of water. Some are burned and need to have their injuries treated. Others are hungry and need food and rest. If the furry patient is too weak to be released right away, it's taken to the hospital—but not a hospital for people. After the wildfires, thousands of animals were treated in veterinary hospitals for wildlife, found in many towns across Australia. The Port Macquarie Koala Hospital even has a special koala ambulance!

Veterinary hospitals offer koalas the best of medical care.

Koala First Aid

One day in November of 2019, an Australian named Roslyn Irwin was walking across a recently burned area when she spotted a koala hobbling across the ground. She could see it was a young female, barely two years old—and it was in trouble. The little koala was wheezing and panting because her lungs had been damaged from breathing smoke. Her fur was singed and black-ened, and there was a huge burn on her back. All four paws were badly burned, too. Roslyn worked with an organization called Friends of the Koala, so she knew how to take action.

How do you give first aid to a koala? First, it needs a long drink of water. The young koala was very dehydrated, and she eagerly sipped from a water bottle. Pain medicine helped to relieve the ache of burned paws. Then the starv-ing animal was given some fresh eucalyptus leaves to munch on. The koala was taken to Currumbin Wildlife Hospital in Queensland, where the staff named her Ember.

At first the veterinarians who worked on Ember weren't sure if she would survive. She was thin and weak, and her burns were serious. Her paws had been damaged by the fire, which

A dehydrated koala gets a drink.

meant she might not be able to grab branches to climb trees.

But Ember kept eating and drinking and regaining her strength, and slowly her injured lungs and paws healed. After several months, she was doing better but wasn't yet strong enough to go back to the wild. She left the hospital and was transferred to a rehabilitation center run by Friends of the Koala. There, she lived in a roomy cage with lots of branches to climb, so she could get her muscles strong again. Weeks passed as she learned to grasp branches firmly and climb with ease.

Marley Christian is a veterinary nurse who watched Ember practicing her climbing day after day. "After months of ongoing treatment and fattening up, this lucky survivor was ready for release," she remembers. "I was in awe; what a survivor!" All the doctors, nurses, and staff who had worked with Ember for half a year crossed their fingers as their young patient was taken to a forested area and released. Would she be able to survive in the wild? They would have to wait to find out.

A School for Koalas

Delungra is a small town in the remote, dry countryside of southeastern Australia. Every morning as the students of Delungra Public School head off to the classroom, part of their morning routine is to carefully check the eucalyptus trees that surround the school building. The sharp-eyed students have gotten really good at spotting koalas. Koalas not only hang out in the branches overhead, they also sometimes climb down and stroll across the schoolyard.

One hot day the students were playing a game of cricket (which is a game played with a ball and bat but is different from baseball) during recess when a koala walked right through the middle of the game! At first the students were thrilled to watch him, but soon they realized that the animal seemed weak and confused. Wildlife rescue volunteers were called, and they realized the koala was very dehydrated. After spending time at the hospital, he was welcomed back to the school grounds and released into the trees. The students named him Buddy.

Buddy helped the people of Delungra realize that life was becoming a lot harder for their furry neighbors. Their town had escaped fire damage, but many of the gum trees around the school had died in the dry years of 2017 to 2020. Koalas were not only having trouble finding food, they were also becoming dehydrated because the leaves on the remaining trees didn't contain enough moisture. Koalas had to climb down to the ground, using up precious energy, to search for water. More and more of the koalas they spotted were showing signs of dehydration or weakness. So students and teachers worked together to come up with an action plan to help the koalas.

The first step was to help the thirsty koalas

reach water easily. How do you make a drinking fountain for koalas? The students chose a particular gum tree that was often visited by the animals. A basin fed by a hose was placed on a high, raised platform right next to the trunk, so the koalas could reach water without leaving the shade and safety of the tree.

The next step was to plant eucalyptus trees to replace the ones that had died. But to grow large numbers of eucalyptus, the students needed seeds, shovels, and other supplies. They also needed a place to plant the seeds and take care of the growing sprouts. Parents and teachers started fundraising on social media, and many people donated. A national news story about their Koala Project helped bring in more funds. Eventually the school received a grant from the state government to build a greenhouse for growing trees. Once the trees are big enough, students will plant them around the school.

Working to save the koalas has become a focus of the whole Delungra community. "It feels really good to just do something," said student Edward Baker, who was in fifth grade when the Koala Project started. "Not just stand there and go, 'Oh, it's so bad, the koalas.'"

Would You Like to Kiss a Koala?

Saving koalas is not only about planting more trees. It's where you plant them that really counts.

The reason so many koalas pass through the Delungra schoolyard is because it's part of a wildlife corridor, which is a pathway between two areas of habitat. To get from one to the other, koalas need trees for rest stops, shade, and snacks on their way. Trees planted in a wildlife corridor act as stepping stones, helping the koalas to pass through the open area safely.

The Australian Koala Foundation has developed a program called the Koala Kiss Project. They've spent years mapping the places where koalas live, and the maps showed that koala habitats are broken up into many small patches, separated by roads, houses, and farms. But in some places, the patches come close to touching each other. These places are called "kiss points."

By encouraging landowners to plant trees at kiss points, important sections of koala habitat could be linked together. This would let the animals travel safely to avoid fire, find food and water, and seek out mates.

Planting new trees is important, but it takes many years before a forest of young trees can produce enough leaves to support a koala

Deborah Tabart of the Australian Koala Foundation hugs a friend.

population. Forests which have never been logged or disturbed by people are important for koala habitats. Creating more national parks and forest preserves would help to protect old-growth forests. Adding new trees to make kiss points could connect these areas to each other.

But kiss points aren't just for koalas. Thousands of other species of Australian wildlife have the same problems of habitat loss as koalas. If enough patches of habitat are linked, it could create a trail hundreds of miles long that humans could enjoy, too, and so could wombats, dingoes, and kookaburras. Turtles could stroll in the shade as kangaroos hop past, endangered parrots flit through the branches, and koalas move from tree to tree.

Would You Like to Borrow a Koala?

Unless you live in Australia, you're not going to spot a koala at school or in your backyard. But not every single koala lives in Australia—some are found in the United States, in California,

Florida, or Ohio. Others make their home in countries like Japan, France, or Portugal. But these animals aren't hanging out in neighborhood trees—the only place to see a koala in these countries is in a zoo.

In the US, the San Diego Zoo has the largest population of captive koalas outside of Australia—approximately twenty of the adorable creatures. They're some of the most popular animals in the zoo, delighting thousands of visitors every year.

In order to give more people the opportunity to get to know—and care—about koalas, the San Diego Zoo loans koalas. Not to individual people—you can't take one home with you—but to other zoos all over the US and in countries around the world.

How does a koala travel from California

to a faraway country? In style! The koalas fly with a care specialist, and the animals aren't down in the plane's baggage hold with the suitcases—they often have their own first-class seat. They don't care for airplane food, so they travel with their own supply of fresh eucalyptus branches to snack on. The zoo borrowing the koalas must have a carefully designed display area that has everything the koalas need to thrive: food, climbing space, and plenty of comfortable perches to doze on.

The Koala Loan Program has allowed people all over the world to have the amazing experience of seeing a live koala. Watching a koala carefully choosing just the right leaves, or seeing a mother hug her joey tight, helps people feel closer to these unique animals and want to help them. The funds that are raised from the koala loans are donated to help preserve koala habitats back in Australia.

The Dreaming

One spring day, Roslyn Irwin was once again taking a walk in the woods. As always, she kept a sharp eye out for koalas in the gum trees, and soon she spotted a mother koala with a tiny joey clinging to her back. Roslyn was thrilled to see that the new mother was Ember! The koala was easy to recognize because of a small orange tag that had been attached to her ear in the hospital.

It was more than a year after Ember had been released into the wild after recovering from her terrible injuries. She looked strong and healthy, climbing through the branches with the curious baby peeking over her shoulder.

Ember and her baby gave new hope to koala

lovers and conservationists. Their story showed that rescuing koalas and releasing them back to the wild can be effective, as long as there is habitat for them to live in. Ember is a symbol that, with lots of help, the koalas can survive.

Centuries ago, there were millions of koalas in trees across the great continent of Australia. We can dream of a day when the forests will be filled with koalas again.

What does the future hold for koalas?

FUN FACTS FOR KOALA FANS

1. If a koala ever happened to walk through a crime scene, detectives might have trouble telling the koala fingerprints from the human ones. Koala fingerprints look almost exactly like human prints.

2. Koalas have front paws that are perfectly adapted for their tree-climbing life. They have two long, skinny thumbs on each of their paws. This gives them an extra-strong grip on branches.

3. Their back paws are handy, too. They have a special claw that's split so that

the koalas can use it as a comb to groom their fur, keeping it clean and smooth.

4. A koala named Midori has celebrated her twenty-fifth birthday in a zoo in Japan. In the wild, koalas probably live about fifteen years on average, but no one knows whether there are koalas older than Midori climbing the gum trees in Australia.

5. Even though they're cute, it's illegal to keep a koala as a pet anywhere in the world. Only licensed zoos, animal hospitals, or scientific organizations can keep koalas in captivity.

6. Unlike other marsupials like kangaroos or wombats, koalas do not have tails.

7. Koalas have sharp front teeth to nip off the tough stems of eucalyptus leaves.

Then their flat back teeth grind the leaves up, chewing very thoroughly to get as much nourishment as possible. Koala jaws are powerful and can give a very hard bite!

8. The original inhabitants of Australia had great respect for koalas, and there are many Aboriginal legends about these animals. Some stories say that koalas magically control the weather, and that disrespecting koalas could cause droughts.

HOW YOU CAN HELP SAVE THE KOALAS

Koalas need the help of all the animal lovers in the world. But how can we save an animal that lives in a faraway land? There are lots of things we can do to help save the koalas if we're willing to get busy!

1. All around the world, May 3 is International Koala Day! Spread the word about koalas and the challenges they face. Maybe you could host a Koala Day event at your school, do a science fair project, or consider working with

an adult to use social media.

2. In Australia, September is Save the Koala Month, and September 30 is Save the Koala Day: a time to focus on helping these famous furry symbols of the land down under.

3. One of the best ways to help endangered wildlife is by raising money to support some of the not-for-profit organizations working to help them. Consider bake sales, raffles, or even a community event sponsored by local businesses. Here are some possibilities for donations:

• You can give to Port Macquarie Koala Hospital to support the Koala Ambulance. Visit KoalaHospital.org.au for more information.

• Support the Australian Koala

Foundation to help the Koala Kiss Project. Head to SaveTheKoala.com to learn more.

- Friends of the Koala works to help injured koalas heal so they can return to the wild. Check out FriendsOfTheKoala.org to find out more.

4. Think you can't raise enough money to make a difference? A donation of about $5 to the Currumbin Wildlife Hospital (where Ember was treated) is enough to plant a eucalyptus tree to feed injured koalas! Go to CurrumbinSanctuary.com .au/Wildlife-Hospital/Tree-To-Me to read more.

5. Adopt Jimmie Jams, Lucy, or Coolabah the koalas. No, you can't bring them

home, but some not-for-profits offer adoption programs. You or your class could symbolically adopt an animal and receive photos and updates on its life. Here are a few organizations that can help you do just that:

- SaveTheKoala.com/Adopt-A-Koala
- LonePineKoalaSanctuary.com /Animal-Sponsorships
- Shop.KoalaHospital.org.au /Collections/Koala-Adoptions
- CurrumbinSanctuary.com.au /Get-Involved/Adopt-An-Animal

6. Check out the website of the Delungra Public School's Koala Project to see photos of the koala water fountain and the eucalyptus greenhouse, and to get some ideas on how your school could get active

to help your local wildlife. Delungra-P
.Schools.NSW.gov.au/Koala-Project.html

7. Wipe for Wildlife! That's the motto of koala
   fans in Australia, who have launched a
   campaign to get people to buy recycled
   toilet paper that is not made from cut-
   ting down eucalyptus trees. When your
   family shops, look for products that are
   made with recycled paper.

8. Is there a koala in your future? If working
   to help animals is your hobby, maybe it
   could become your job! Research ways to
   pursue a career helping wildlife all over
   the world. Here are some places to start:

   • The Wildlife Society: Wildlife.org
     /Next-Generation/Career-
     Development/Careers/

   • LiveAbout.com: LiveAbout.com

/Careers-With-Wildlife-125918

- National Wildlife Federation: NWF .org/About-Us/Careers

9. Write to your representatives in government and urge them to take strong action to protect endangered species. Generally, their contact information is easily available on the internet. You can go to House.gov to find out who your representative is. Ask them how they are working to protect wildlife.

10. VOTE! One of the best ways to help wildlife is to support political candidates who support environmental protection. Register to vote as soon as you're old enough and encourage your family and friends to vote with the environment in mind.

ACKNOWLEDGMENTS

Thanks to all the koala lovers who are working so hard to save these amazing animals! Special thanks to Deborah Tabart for reading over the manuscript and sharing her love of koalas.

REFERENCES

Australian Koala Foundation. 2022. "Koala Threats." savethekoala.com/about-koalas/koala-threats/.

Australian Koala Foundation. "30% of All Australia's Remaining Koalas Lost in Just Three Years—New Population Figures Show a Three-Year Decline as High as 41% in NSW/ACT & 37% in QLD." September 20, 2021. savethekoala.com/wp-content/uploads/2021/09/MediaRelease_Koalapopulations.pdf.

"Background & History." IUCN Red List of Threatened Species: About. International Union for Conservation of Nature. iucnredlist.org/about/background-history.

"Bushfire Survivor Koala Ember Spotted in the Wild
with Joey." News and Events: News. Friends of
the Koala, September 8, 2021. friendsofthekoala
.org/bushfire-survivor-koala-ember-spotted-in
-the-wild-with-joey/.

Castagnino, Romina. "How to Help Koalas Recover
after Australia's Fires? Q&A with Rebecca
Montague-Drake." Mongabay, March 19, 2020.
news.mongabay.com/2020/03/how-to-help
-koalas-recover-after-australias-fires-qa-with
-rebecca-montague-drake/.

Common Ground Team. "The Significance of Koalas
for First Nations People." Common Ground.
commonground.org.au/learn/the-significance
-of-koalas-for-first-nations-people.

Currumbin Wildlife Hospital. 2022. "Currumbin
Wildlife Hospital Leading the Way in Urgent
Koala Research." Currumbin Wildlife Hospital.
currumbinsanctuary.com.au/wildlife-hospital
/koala-chlamydia-vaccine-research-trial.

Delungra Public School. Koala Project. NSW
    Department of Education. delungra-p.schools
    .nsw.gov.au/koala-project.html.

Eszterhas, Suzi. *Koala Hospital*. Toronto, ON: Owlkids
    Books, 2015.

Flannery, Tim. *The Future Eaters: An Ecological
    History of the Australasian Lands and People.*
    New York, NY: Grove Press, 2002.

International Fund for Animal Welfare. "What It's
    Like to Rehabilitate a Koala." About IFAW:
    News: Blog. International Fund for Animal Wel-
    fare, June 17, 2021. ifaw.org/journal/rehabilitate
    -koala-answers.

Pickrell, John. *Flames of Extinction: The Race to Save
    Australia's Threatened Wildlife.* Washington, DC:
    Island Press, 2021.

Port Macquarie Koala Hospital. "Loss of Habitat."
    2022. koalahospital.org.au/loss-of-habitat.html.

San Diego Zoo Wildlife Alliance. "Koala." Animals
    and Plants. San Diego Zoo Wildlife Alliance.
    animals.sandiegozoo.org/animals/koala.

Sheil, Donal. "The Primary School Students Saving
    Their Tiny Town's Koala Population." ABC
    News. Australian Broadcasting Corporation,
    October 10, 2020. abc.net.au/news/2020-10-11
    /school-growing-trees-save-koala-drought
    -bushfire/12743570.

Sranko, George. "Koala Brain—Why Are Koalas
    the Dumbest Animal? How Being Dumb Can Be
    Smart." BioGeoPlanet. biogeoplanet.com
    /koala-brains-dumbest-mammal/.

Tabart, Deborah. *Koala Stories*. Photography by
    Suzi Eszterhas. Kenmore, QLD: Ghost Cat Pty
    Ltd, 2015.

ANITA SANCHEZ is especially fascinated by plants and animals that no one loves and by the unusual, often ignored wild places of the world. Her award-winning books sing the praises of the unappreciated: dandelions, poison ivy, tarantulas, mud puddles. Her goal is to make young readers excited about science and nature. Many years of fieldwork and teaching outdoor classes have given her firsthand experience in introducing students to the wonders of the natural world.

Photo by George Steele

You can visit Anita Sanchez online at
AnitaSanchez.com
and follow her on Twitter
@ASanchezAuthor

CHELSEA CLINTON is the author of the #1 *New York Times* bestseller *She Persisted: 13 American Women Who Changed the World*; *She Persisted Around the World: 13 Women Who Changed History*; *She Persisted in Sports: American Olympians Who Changed the Game*; *Don't Let Them Disappear: 12 Endangered Species Across the Globe*; *It's Your World: Get Informed, Get Inspired & Get Going!*; *Start Now!: You Can Make a Difference*; with Hillary Clinton, *Grandma's Gardens* and *The Book of Gutsy Women: Favorite Stories of Courage and Resilience*; and, with Devi Sridhar, *Governing Global Health: Who Runs the World and Why?* She is also the Vice Chair of the Clinton Foundation, where she works on many initiatives, including those that help empower the next generation of leaders. She lives in New York City with her husband, Marc, their children and their dog, Soren.

Photo courtesy of the author

You can follow Chelsea Clinton on Twitter
@ChelseaClinton
or on Facebook at
Facebook.com/ChelseaClinton

DON'T MISS MORE BOOKS IN THE

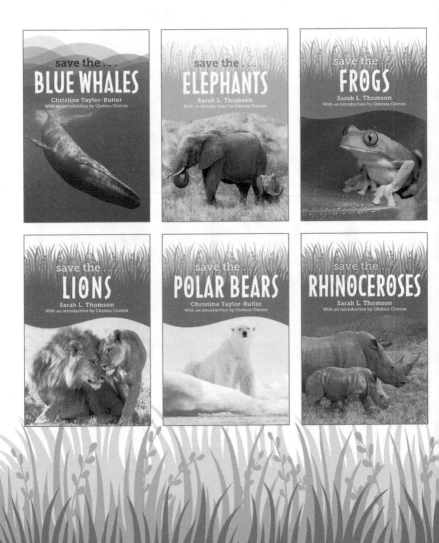

save the . . .
BLUE WHALES
Christine Taylor-Butler
With an introduction by Chelsea Clinton

save the . . .
ELEPHANTS
Sarah L. Thomson
With an introduction by Chelsea Clinton

save the . . .
FROGS
Sarah L. Thomson
With an introduction by Chelsea Clinton

save the . . .
LIONS
Sarah L. Thomson
With an introduction by Chelsea Clinton

save the . . .
POLAR BEARS
Christine Taylor-Butler
With an introduction by Chelsea Clinton

save the . . .
RHINOCEROSES
Sarah L. Thomson
With an introduction by Chelsea Clinton

save the . . . SERIES!